MW00698669

Fanny Waterman

On Piano Teaching and Performing

'A love affair with the piano and pianists'

NEW EDITION

First published in 1983 by Faber Music Ltd
This revised edition first published in 2006 by Faber Music Ltd
Bloomsbury House 74–77 Great Russell Street London WC1B 3DA
cover photograph © reproduced courtesy of the *Yorkshire Post*
Typesetting by Agnesi Text
Printed in England by Caligraving Ltd

All rights reserved

© 1983 and 2006 by Fanny Waterman

ISBN10: 0-571-52519-9
EAN13: 978-0-571-52519-5

Contents

Other books available from Faber Music
by Fanny Waterman and Marion Harewood

Piano Lessons (Books 1, 2 and 3)
Piano Playtime (Books 1 and 2)
Piano Playtime Studies
Piano Progress (Books 1 and 2)
Piano Progress Studies (Books 1 and 2)
Recital Repertoire (Books 1 and 2)
Two at the Piano (duet)
Young Pianist's Repertoire (Books 1 and 2)
Piano for Pleasure (Books 1 and 2)
Me and My Piano (Parts 1 and 2)
Me and My Piano. Repertoire
Me and My Piano. Superscales
Me and My Piano Duets (Books 1 and 2)
Merry Christmas Carols
Animal Magic (piano exercises)
Nursery Rhyme Time

To buy Faber Music publications or to find out about
the full range of titles available please contact
your local music retailer or Faber Music sales enquiries:

Faber Music Limited,
Burnt Mill, Elizabeth Way, Harlow, CM20 2HX, England
Tel: +44 (0)1279 82 89 82   Fax: +44 (0)1279 82 89 83
sales@fabermusic.com   www.fabermusic.com

Preface

Many years ago I was invited by the Royal Society of Arts in London to give the Tolansky Memorial Lecture, and chose as my subject the preparation of the young pianist for the concert platform. The first edition of this book grew out of that lecture, stimulated in particular by a series of piano master-class programmes – entitled *Piano Progress* – which I was commissioned to prepare for screening on Channel 4. That manuscript would not have gone to press without the invaluable help of my husband Geoffrey de Keyser, and publisher, Martin Kingsbury.

This second edition has been updated to reflect the experiences I have had over the last twenty years since the book was first published, and includes further thoughts and words of advice for all musicians. Many people have invited me in recent times to talk about the world of competitions, to which I have devoted a great deal of my professional life, and the book has therefore also been expanded to include a chapter on this subject. A new appendix includes some of the thought-provoking and often inspiring *Rules and Maxims for Young Pianists* of Robert Schumann, many of which, although written nearly two hundred years ago, are still startlingly fresh and relevant for today's musicians.

Of all professions, I regard teaching to be the most important. One cannot become a doctor, lawyer, engineer, chef or joiner without someone to guide and inspire us. Teachers have tremendous influence over our lives from our earliest days. This chain of influence is infinite.

This book is dedicated to Geoffrey, who was my rock and inspiration for fifty-seven years, with love and gratitude.

Fanny Waterman

DAME FANNY WATERMAN DBE
November 2005

Dear Fanny,

It was such a pleasure to share a few minutes with you and so very good of you to write so warmly after the concert in Cologne. I think your little book on piano teaching contains most valuable nuggets of advice and proceeds from very great experience and a very concerned one. Everything you say about the lesson format, about musicianship, the clues in the composition (I have always felt that studying a composition is very much like a piece of detective work) couldn't be more true! I also agree with you about bar lines – they are a great danger and too often represent prison bars!

Devotedly,
YEHUDI [MENUHIN]
13 December 1983

––––––

Dame Fanny and I used to meet on juries many years ago. We are fellow Yorkshire women and I like to think we hit it off in a big way, feeling very much on the same wavelength about musical matters in general; I thought she had more common sense, honesty and integrity than anyone I had ever met; I still do.

Her wisdom leaps out on every page of this book; she misses nothing; her standards are meticulously high and she expects the best even from the youngest pupil. Every step is described simply but with devastating accuracy and some of the ways in which she gets over an idea are simplicity itself not to say endearing; but they work.

No one could help but develop an enduring love for the piano or better understand what it takes to achieve the standard of excellence she expects; it is all done with such knowledge, clarity and sheer kindness.

The adjectives I use are nothing more nor less than a description of her as a person – she embodies all the qualities she looks for in her pupils. I wish I had known her when I began the piano at the age of thirteen.

As a sure guide to every aspect of teaching and performing, this book is a gem. So is she.

DAME JANET BAKER CH DBE
January 2006

Introduction

In 1943 a 'brilliantly gifted pianist and musician' left the Royal College of Music, London, after studying with Tobias Matthay and Cyril Smith, two of the finest teachers of the day. That student had won most of the important awards for pianists at the College and, at the end of her time there, was invited to play at a Promenade Concert with Sir Henry Wood and the BBC Symphony Orchestra. What more auspicious beginning to a career as a concert pianist could there be?

Let me confess that I was that young pianist. As with so many young artists – the majority perhaps – things did not turn out quite as I had expected. I found my vocation was teaching – my true vocation, that is, and not just second best to performing (perhaps fulfilling Cyril Smith's prophecy that I 'would be an inspiration to [my] pupils'). I then began to ask myself how I could draw on my experience as a performer-pianist to benefit others and to help them meet the challenges to be faced in the art of piano playing and performance.

The three aspects of musical training which I believe to be of paramount importance are: learning to be a craftsman, learning to be a musician, and becoming an artist.

The first and most important step in becoming a fine pianist is to learn the CRAFT; that is, to master every technical aspect of piano playing by learning *how*: how to play a scale at speed with each note of equal brilliance or pearly delicacy (as in Mozart's Sonatas); how to play trills and repeated notes dynamically controlled to suit the mood of the music (as in Beethoven); how to develop a wrist staccato resembling the vertical action of a piston; how to master the art of tone production and pedalling (the perpetual challenge of how to make the piano sing, demanded by all composers, especially Schubert, Schumann and Chopin); how to achieve powerful octaves (Liszt), accurate skips and perfect co-ordination between the hands; how to balance parts when playing more than one melody at once in polyphonic music ... all these, and a host of other technical details, must be mastered.

Mastering such musical details will absorb the true pianist from their first lesson to their very last performance. Although work on problems of physical technique will occupy only a fraction of the pianist's working day (some being used simply for limbering up), it is nevertheless a vital part of their efforts to produce the most apt and beautiful sounds and convincing interpretations, which is the aim of all technical work. Craftsmanship or 'technique' cannot be created in a vacuum. I have never been able to accept that there is a dividing line between technique and the two other aspects of training – musicianship and artistry. With these three aims we embrace a limitless and elusive field where each individual's imagination and personality have an essential role to play.

My approach is to help the pupil to explore the artistic essence of the work, and to strive for *their* ideal interpretation. No amount of 'technique' in the sense of a precise and faultless rendering of the notes, velocity, bravura, etc., will produce a fine interpretation. When my pupils play a passage accurately but without feeling, I tell them they sound like a musical typewriter. Only when technical practice is combined with the study of the *meaning* behind the notes will it lead to a musically artistic performance. Let us remember that composers of yesteryear would not have had the benefit of our modern-day computers and music software ... each of the millions of notes they wrote were precious to them and will have been painstakingly considered before their quill was dipped into ink and committed to manuscript.

So now let us move on to the second aspect of training: MUSICIANSHIP. From the very beginning every young musician – on whatever instrument – must learn how to shape and colour a phrase; then how to play it in relation both to the next phrase and to the previous phrase; how to join several phrases together rhythmically, so that a large section – for example, an exposition or development – is fused together; and, finally, how to build together large sections to give the piece or movement rhythmic unity as one architectural whole. The teacher must help the young musician to achieve this by developing a strong rhythmic sense and pulse, so that even the shortest note is in its correct 'time-spot'. When this rhythmic understanding is secure, they must learn to use rubato, where speeds fluctuate – almost imperceptibly in Classical music, more markedly with Romantic music and with certain twentieth-century composers. In acquiring musicianship, the study of style and knowledge of composers' lives and times, what instruments were used and how they sounded, is vitally important. *Respiration* in the use of rubato reveals the fascinating differences between every performer, and marks each with their own individual stamp: it is almost impossible to teach. This rubato must be flexible and not set in stone; it should vary from performance to performance.

How can a pianist equipped with technical virtuosity, deep musical knowledge and sensitivity blossom into an artist? This third and vital step is also impossible to teach. ARTISTRY is the one quality that, I believe, is innate and therefore cannot be taught but only stimulated.

I shall return in more detail to these three aspects of studying the piano – craftsmanship, musicianship and artistry. But before doing this, it may be helpful if I outline my own lesson format.

Lesson Format

Every lesson at every stage must be a musical injection, so that the student returns home, refreshed and bursting with new ideas and thoughts. Most young beginners can concentrate for only a short time, so their lessons last approximately half an hour. Before introducing any new material, we will go through the previous week's work, with marks given for each item and an overall percentage. If they get 80 per cent or over they get a blue star; 90 per cent or over, a gold star. And ten lessons each with a star will win them a prize. I am a great believer in incentives. Better results can be obtained in this way than by telling an eight-year-old that if they practise every day, they *might* one day become a great pianist.

A detailed plan for daily practice, including any specific musical ideas or pointers, is always written down in a notebook. A short legible report at the end of each lesson, commenting on concentration and absorption of new ideas – i.e. what has been *achieved* in the lesson – will be of great motivation to the pupil (with a longer summary at the end of a term). I find that recording the lesson with a tape recorder or mini-disc is invaluable as a reminder of wrong notes, wrong tempi, wrong rhythmic patterns, lack of dynamic contrast and so on. As the relationship between pupil and teacher is based on constructive comments and in partnership, the discussions at the lesson will provide invaluable food for thought over the week. It can also act as an invaluable aid to hold the pupil's interest during the week of practising between lessons. I also encourage a parent to be present at lessons. Parents then share the experience of the child's lesson and, in recalling the points raised by the teacher, can supervise practice at home and play a vital role in the child's progress and enjoyment of the piano. (I am sometimes asked how I choose my pupils, and I reply: I don't choose the pupils, I choose the parents!)

At the first lesson I give the young pianist a list of Ten Musical Commandments. These vary somewhat according to their age but the principal ones are as follows:

1   Keep your back straight and your fingers rounded;

2   Practise regularly every day;

3   Before you start playing any unfamiliar music, clap the rhythm counting the beats aloud;

4   Choose fingering most suited to your hand, write it on the music in pencil and try not to change it;

5   Hands separately before hands together;

6   Practise slowly before playing up to speed;

7   When practising, correct any mistake on the spot and play the passage several times correctly before going on or back;

8   Play any piece with a strong pulse throughout first, before introducing any rubato or rhythmic freedom;

9   Follow *all* the composer's markings, making the difference between the six dynamic levels (*pp, p, mp, mf, f, ff*);

10 Listen to *every* sound you make on the piano, and strive for the most beautiful sound. (The analogy of a musical post-office can help here: just as a letter moves from place to place, so the creation of sound moves from your fingertips, through your body, to your ears and brain, backwards and forwards.)

The normal lesson time for older children is about one hour. This gives time for technical work – Czerny studies, for example, and basic exercises that I have evolved over the years – one or two pieces in different styles and from different periods, sight reading and aural tests. Each piece will give rise to technical work on such details as fingering, tone-production and phrasing. One or two pieces are studied in great depth over a period of many weeks in preparation for a performance – I believe that a piece is not really learnt until it has been performed either in public or to family and friends at home. The teacher should always look for opportunities to arrange informal concerts in front of other young musicians and their parents, since these provide a valuable stimulus and incentive. Even at this early stage, the teacher should stress the importance of body language and taking command of the performing situation: after entering the room amid applause and bowing naturally, sit down at the piano with hands at rest for a second or two before finding the correct notes in each hand and starting to play. This will help to prevent false starts.

Advanced students are encouraged to listen to each others' lessons, which last one or two hours (or indeed more) depending on the amount of work prepared. I rarely work on pre-prepared exercises, scales or studies in these lessons, but I do concentrate on any technical problems that arise in the course of the lesson. I ask the student to bring a piece of their own choice: it is important that they play something for which they have a natural love and affinity. I may, however, offer suggestions as to what they should study next, in order to help them to build up a balanced repertoire from which they can later choose their recital programmes.

At the beginning of the lesson I ask the student to perform the whole piece or movement without any interruption, and from memory. Whatever mishaps occur in this performance they must carry on – for they must learn quickly to cover up mistakes and recover from memory slips. This is, of course, quite the reverse of their quick reaction to making mistakes when practising at home. Then they must stop, recall exactly what happened, think critically why the mistake was made, correct it, play the correct version several times, and only then link the entire passage from before and with what follows. (A tape recorder can be invaluable for exposing both a technical fault and the factors that lead up to it.) It is said that if Toscanini's players didn't deliver at a rehearsal he would explode; but if there was a slip-up at a performance, this was the human factor: it could happen to anyone at any time and there were never any post-mortem recriminations.

Memorising is, I believe, something everyone can do if is tackled in the right way – unlike, for example, sight-reading, for which some pianists have a natural flair. First, there is the tactile sense by which the pianist absorbs a specific fingering pattern over a period of weeks. Then there is the photographic memory: for example, knowing that on the score, on the top left-hand side, there is the 'end of the second subject'. Seeing this in their mind's eye the pianist can, as it were, turn over the pages in their imagination as they are playing. Then there is the aural memorising – knowing what sounds follow next and how to find them on the keyboard. I never say to my pupils, 'Memorise this piece by next week', because memorising should not be forced but come naturally out of the concentrated, intelligent effort that is required in studying any piece. Memorising away from the keyboard is an extra tool for security. And of course, one must be very careful when altering fingering: this must never be the day before a recital. It takes some time to absorb new fingering, and one must take into account the sense of stress that generally occurs before a performance in public. (In the army, 'order, counter-order and disorder' are words of advice given to young officers!)

When the student is playing in the lesson I will follow the score, and make notes and comments in it. I insist on good editions with as little editing as possible, although it is always interesting to examine the editions of master pianists and teachers such as Schnabel (his edition of the Beethoven Sonatas) or Cortot (Chopin's *Etudes*). At the end of the student's performance, I will always find something to praise and then make general critical comments. The real work then begins: on *every* note of *every* bar of *every* phrase in the greatest detail. The student must be able to start from any beat of any bar (eventually from memory). The opening phrase of a piece could absorb an entire lesson – for instance, the first chord of Beethoven's Fourth Piano Concerto, or the precise rhythmic pattern in the *pianissimo* opening of his 'Appassionata' Sonata, or the relationship of sound and silence in the first bars of Liszt's B minor Sonata.

I will try the passage myself several times in different ways, and together we discover the approach that the student prefers. They, in turn, will try the passage several times and the process of exploration and discovery continues until *they* have clarified this interpretation for themselves. These reciprocal exchanges may go on for some time. As part of the process of exploration, I will comment on details such as the balance between the hands, the voicing of chords, polyphonic clarity, sequential phrases, the unobtrusive emergence of one chord or phrase from another, the mood of the passage and respiration. Besides playing, I will also demonstrate by singing, conducting, making up words to fit the music, capturing its mood with a quotation from a piece of poetry, even making them dance, if necessary. This process is applied to successive passages until the entire piece or movement has been explored and a unified performance has emerged. This can take up several lessons.

In the next chapter I return to the first aspect of musical training – craftsmanship or 'technique' – in greater detail.

Craftsmanship

Technical development and musical development should go hand in hand – a great painter, an actor, a doctor, scientist or composer must know 'how to', and this is where technique begins.

No two hands, as the police well know, are the same. In the early stages of learning the piano, great thought must be given to the most comfortable fingering of a passage, with the proviso that it also produces the best sound. Pupils, I find, all too readily accept the 'ready-made' fingering printed in their music. If they do so, I will ask them how well they remember the hand of, say, Mr Harold Craxton. Did he have long slender fingers or short chubby ones? They give me a blank stare in reply, until I point out to them that the fingering has been done by Harold Craxton to suit *his* hand, and he certainly had quite a different hand from theirs. *Their* fingering must be 'made to measure' and worked out with the help of the teacher. To show the pupil how hands and fingers vary in size and shape, the teacher should trace in pencil the outline of their own hand and the pupil's on a sheet of paper – or inside the cover of the music – and compare the two.

Craftsmanship must start with tone-production. Even on a single note we can play from the softest to the loudest sound; we can produce a large tone without hardness and a *pianissimo* that will carry to the last row of the top gallery. I like to explain this tonal variety to my pupils by comparing it to the artist's palette of colours. Just as there are many different shades of blue – for example, powder blue, turquoise, navy blue, sky blue, Wedgwood blue and pacific blue – so there are many different nuances of piano tone. Much has been written and said about tone-production and I would like initially to draw attention to a few important considerations.

First, pianists must learn how to listen to themselves – how to listen, that is, to the quality of every sound they produce. Good tone-production comes, in the first place, from having the right sound in your ear so that you can recognise it when you hear it. The teacher can help here by demonstrating at the piano the range of possibilities, and by constantly encouraging the student to assess whether a particular sound being produced matches the sound they desire. When they have heard themselves produce a really fine tone once, they will never forget it. I sometimes ask my pupils and audiences at masterclasses whether they would rather hear a mediocre pianist on a fine piano or a fine pianist on a mediocre instrument, and they immediately know the answer. I remind them that, unlike other instrumentalists, pianists cannot carry their own piano around with them. But they can carry and remember their own sound by having the ability to cajole that sound out of even an indifferent instrument. (Sometimes they may find themselves having to play on a piano that is worse than indifferent, in which case I tell them to do the best they can: 'What can't be cured must be endured.')

This leads on directly to the second element in tone-production, the question of 'touch'. It is vital for the pianist to understand that the character and volume of sound depends on the speed at which the piano key descends to the key bed. To control the speed of key descent is to control the volume. It is also to control the tonal colour, since the 'mix' of partials caused by a forcible impact of hammer on string is different from that produced by a gentler one. I show my pupils that the key can be depressed by only a quarter of an inch, and that all types of tone must be produced within this small depth.

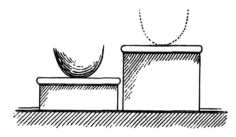

If the key is depressed very slowly, no sound at all is emitted. By quickening the descent just fractionally, the thinnest thread of sound can be produced. The pianist must feel the exact finger movement required, which of course will vary from one piano to another. At the other extreme the hand, with a loose wrist, can come swiftly down on a key from a height to produce a really full, strong sonority. Between these extremes come the many speeds of key descent that yield the full palette of tonal colours.

To make the point clearer to my younger pupils, I ask them to imagine that they have a rubber ball in their hand. If it slips gently out of their hand down to the ground, it will produce much less sound than if it were bounced with vigour. They soon get the message, and enjoy producing sounds at different dynamic levels and in the differing moods associated with each level. This is exploited in one of the first five-finger tunes I give to beginners:

Lullaby *If you play this softly and die away at the end, it will sound like a lullaby.*

March *If you play this loudly and finish with a bold ending, it will sound like a march.*

Tone quality is, of course, also affected by the position of the fingers. Bright passage-work requires well-rounded fingers (joints well bent), so that only the fingertips are in contact with the keys. For fuller tone, the fingers should be less rounded, i.e. slightly flatter (joints less bent), so that the fleshy cushion of the fingertip is used. This can be demonstrated by tapping a table first with the tip of a pencil and then with the flat side of its full length; also try playing imaginary notes on your bare arm – first with the fingertips (well-rounded fingers), then with the fleshy cushion of the fingertips (fingers flatter) – so that you can feel the difference.

The use of the sustaining and *Una Corda* pedals is an important element in tone-production, and I will come to this later in this section.

The last general point concerns the wrist. A stiff, tense wrist is enemy number one, producing a hard tone and inhibiting any good tone-

17

production. On the other hand, a flexible wrist acts as a shock-absorber. In full tone it allows the weight of the arm to be transmitted to the fingers without the percussive accented bumps and thumps that otherwise are so frequently produced. In fast passage-work it should not be too yielding, but through its flexibility gives essential elastic support to the fingers. Of course, the wrist will never be flexible if the arm and shoulder are tense. So it is equally important that the arm is relaxed and the shoulder down, never hunched.

Before tackling any passage-work, we must learn to play two connected notes with the same power and evenness, backwards and forwards in a see-saw movement, transferring the weight from one finger to another, keeping the arm relaxed and the shoulder down (see the See-Saw Exercise below). We should always play on the tips of the fingers (so nails must be short), and keep the fingers rounded, with the joints well bent. If I find any tendency towards straightening the fingers, I ask the pupil to try running with straight legs and then normally, bending the knees: the point is quickly made. Overlapping of adjacent notes must be avoided, as it blurs the sound.

See-Saw Exercise

The same principles should be applied to longer studies – Czerny's studies from *School of Velocity* are invaluable for this purpose. All fingers should be placed in the middle of each key; this helps to avoid split notes from the start. It is important to give the weakest 4th finger special attention or it will produce a limp sound in comparison with the stronger fingers, especially the thumb and the 3rd finger. The pupil should try playing a scale up and down the piano as legato as possible, using the 3rd and 4th fingers exclusively. The secret is to keep the knuckles arched, to raise the fingers as little as possible in moving from note to note, and not to raise the arm at all. Make sure there is no stiffening in the arm or the shoulder.

We should note, in passing, that the 4th finger's lack of independence stems from the fact that its tendons have connections with those of its two adjoining fingers. We therefore have less muscular control over that specific finger. (Though it is unlikely that the cradle devised by Schumann was the primary cause of his celebrated problems with the 4th finger, we should take heed and not allow exercises to continue in a condition of strain.) Schnabel's brilliant fingering suggestions omitting the 4th finger in scale passages and proceeding from the 5th to the 3rd are worth consideration.

In approaching passage-work and scales, we must be conscious of the relative nature of speed and time. In everyday life a second is the shortest space of time in general use. But musicians must train themselves to think in fractions of a second – a half, a quarter, an eighth, even a sixteenth of a second. A scale played with a note per second will sound slow. Played twice as fast (each note half a second), it is still too slow for most passage-work. Played twice as fast again (each note a quarter of a second), it is at a moderate speed. Halve this time again, and we have now arrived at the approximate speed of the semiquavers/sixteenth-notes in a Mozart allegro. There is still the possibility of halving the time yet again to produce timings of a sixteenth of a second and even shorter, the kind of split-second timings that all musicians must eventually master and control in their playing, especially in polyphonic music.

One of the chief difficulties occurring in passage-work and scales is, of course, the passage of the thumb under the hand (ascending in the right hand, descending in the left) and the passage of the hand over the thumb (descending in the right hand, ascending in the left). The thumb enjoys more muscular power and freedom of movement than any of the other fingers. It not only can move in the opposite direction to them but also functions as a pivot on which the hand can move laterally in either direction. These facilities are exploited in the thumb exercises I give my pupils, in the key of each of the scales they learn. In these exercises, holding the elbow against the side of the body helps to prevent the arm jutting out sideways each time the thumb passes under the hand.

Thumb Exercises

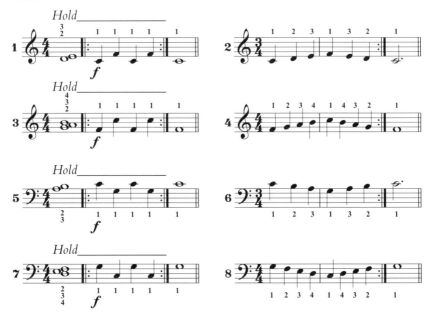

There are very few complete ascending and descending scales in the great works we study. Yes, the opening of Beethoven's Third Piano Concerto has three ascending scales, and Chopin's Prelude in B flat minor Op. 28 No. 16 has complete or nearly complete scales in almost all of its 46 bars. But, on the whole, we have to play *fragments* of scales. Breaking up scales into fragments, both note-by-note and beat-by-beat, is therefore often a valuable exercise (as is starting from the middle of a quick passage with the correct finger):

Breaking up: *Note by note*

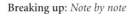

Breaking up: *Beat by beat*

The same technique can be applied to each successive degree of the scale, using the 'key-note' fingerings. Another useful exercise is to play scales in different rhythms and with different dynamics: for example, soft and *leggiero*, loud and *con brio*, starting *f* and getting softer (diminuendo), starting *p* and getting louder (crescendo).* We must learn to grade the tone from *pp* to *ff*, to play both slowly and quickly, legato and staccato. I expect even my youngest pupils to enlarge their musical palette of colours by differentiating between the following six dynamic levels: *pianissimo* (*pp*), *piano* (*p*), *mezzopiano* (*mp*), *mezzoforte* (*mf*), *forte* (*f*) and *fortissimo* (*ff*).

The value of such an approach to scales is twofold: students are introduced to differing types of passage-work they will find in the pieces they study, and at the same time they are provided with models for practising those problematic passages they encounter and will have to master in the pieces they are studying. I believe that the formal practising of scales for only technical reasons has little value and can, indeed, have a numbing effect on students' concentration and listening capacity. They would do better to spend their time in extending their repertoire and applying the 'breaking-up' technique to the fast passage-work in the pieces they learn. It is always helpful to think of such passages as slow melodies played fast, and for this reason I encourage students to sing quick passages slowly so as to focus their hearing on each note in turn, especially in low bass notes.

Similar considerations apply to arpeggios and broken chords. The student should aim for evenness of tone, keeping the wrists flexible and free to move laterally. To help them to get the feel of the different distances of different intervals, they should put the thumb note down silently and play aloud the notes on either side – each with its correct fingering. Once again, holding the elbow against the side (even holding a book under their arm) helps to prevent the arm from jerkily jutting out each time the thumb passes under the hand. There are a number of Czerny studies to help pupils with this problem, while for advanced students the Chopin Study Op. 10 No. 1 is excellent.

I referred earlier to trills, which in my experience always require special attention. In the first place, a trill must consist of two separate notes, not

* These are set out in the Appendix in *Piano Lessons Book Two* and *Book Three*.

one blurred sound. The see-saw and two-note exercise is the one to practise here, slowly at first and then building up the speed. Vary the fingering by using 1st and 2nd, 2nd and 3rd and so on, first on adjacent black notes, then on adjacent white notes, then on adjacent black and white notes. Play also at different dynamic levels and then introduce crescendos, diminuendos, accelerandos and ritardandos. Differing combinations of these elements will be required in differing musical contexts – from the bravura of the final bars of a concerto cadenza to the dream-like quality of a filigree passage in a slow Chopin Nocturne. Practising with a metronome sometimes helps to keep trills rhythmic – and the breaking-up method is as vital here as with scales. As so often in piano playing, singing the written notes is also helpful to establish their relationship with each other and reveal their melodic content. Ends of trills frequently evaporate in a melée of mush. The remedy is to start on the previous beat and play to the last note of the bar – *not* the first note of the next bar – and wait there, listening to check that the hands are still exactly together. When a trill is accompanied by an Alberti bass, there is often a tendency to accent the principal beats too strongly, so care must be taken to avoid such over-accentuation. However, one must be aware of the punctuality of the pulse.

The acquisition of a good octave technique is vitally important, as this writing often occurs in the piano repertoire, thickening the bass and providing a solid foundation, or adding steely brilliance to the treble. (Octaves in the lower register have a particularly important function in that their upper partials reinforce the treble by adding increased resonance.) A pianist with large hands can take octaves in their stride, so long as the wrists remain loose but the fingertips are firm. For accuracy in octave playing the student should practise with the 5th finger alone, and with the thumb alone. Where the repertoire and specific passage-work demands it, they may also practise hands together – 5th finger of right hand; thumb of left, and so on. For those with small hands, I stress the importance of stretching exercises between the fingers every day of their lives – without overdoing it, of course. Even the smallest increase in the extension of their hand will help prevent tightening up and give them a large increase in the repertoire they can tackle. The following exercises I have found helpful and each teacher can work out further examples:

Stretching Exercises

Skips can be another technical problem. A student may practise a difficult skip for hours and it will barely improve; encourage them to use their brains, however, and it is easily improved. I point out that a wide skip involves moving your whole arm, and only if you move it as quickly as possible just above the keys can you arrive in time to play at the other end. But I would go one better than punctuality: if you have to reach notes at the top of the piano, and your journey starts at the bottom, get there *before* you're due. (Nelson attributed whatever success he had in life to his habit of arriving half an hour early for every appointment; we can also learn from Ford's famous quote in Shakespeare's *The Merry Wives of Windsor*: 'Better three hours too soon than a minute too late.') This means practising moving your arm horizontally as quickly as you can to the position required for the next note – but don't play it; that's a waste of time at the moment. Check that the finger is above the correct note. Then, with any luck, at the next attempt you will master the leap straight off.

We now come to the most difficult problem facing the pianist – how to make a primarily percussive instrument 'sing'. Listening, hearing and assessing are vital in this skill; however, there are also three possible techniques the pianist can turn to:

1 Intentional overlapping of notes in a melody;
2 Adjusting the balance of tone between different parts – between melody and accompaniment, between the voices in contrapuntal writing, and so on;
3 Using the sustaining pedal.

These three techniques are not, of course, mutually exclusive and can be exploited simultaneously. Let us briefly consider each of them.

The overlapping technique consists of holding a note fractionally longer than its written value, so that the sound minutely overlaps with the succeeding note or notes. This technique can be applied to any legato passage in music (even scales or fast passage-work), but is most easily appreciated in and applied to disjunct melodic intervals as can be seen in the following example:

Play:

Then remove the pauses and shorten the second of each pair of tied notes so that only a fractional overlap occurs. Split-second timing is here the secret of welding the sounds together and of producing in this way an even, *cantabile* tone. This resembles the vibrato of stringed instruments.

Split-second timing is similarly required to achieve the differentiated syntheses of sounds that are the essence of 'balance'. This works in two ways. First, as we saw earlier, the speed and weight with which the piano key is depressed determines the character and volume of the sound. Balancing the tone, either between the two hands or between principal and subsidiary notes played by a single hand, is therefore a function of the speed of key descent. But it is also a matter of differential timing, in that any note gains prominence and has a life of its own if played a micro-second before other notes are sounded with it. One way of achieving this is to straighten very slightly the finger playing the melody note, to arrive a micro-second earlier than the supporting note or chord, while keeping the other fingers well bent. I need hardly say that this trick of the trade must be handled with great discretion, and must never be exaggerated, but the technique is particularly useful to bring out and sustain one or more parts in contrapuntal music or a melodic line in chordal textures.

Take, for example, a three-part invention. One can bring out the middle part by playing every note fractionally before the top part, so that whenever the sounds coincide, the middle part will have the first aural impact on the listener. Then, if one plays the top part *louder* than the middle part, one will be able to bring that out as well. The beauty of it is that, having dealt in this way with two parts, the third assumes an identity of its own, if only by its apparent subservience to the other two. Such an approach can lead to the clarity of articulation required in all contrapuntal music from Bach to Liszt and on into the twentieth-century repertoire.

Tchaikovsky's *Chorus* from his Children's Album Op. 39 (see page 26) provides an example of a melodic line that must emerge from a chordal texture. The opening chords can be practised as indicated.

The sustaining pedal is one of the piano's greatest assets (Chopin called it 'the soul of the piano'). Yet its use is so subtle that it is one of the most difficult techniques to teach and to master.

We must first be aware that the sustaining pedal not only prolongs the sound of a note and allows successive notes to be joined through their overlapping with each other; it also enriches the sound by adding an aura of vibrations and harmonics and thus places at the player's disposal an important means of colouring the tone.

The mechanism is familiar enough. Normally all strings are damped, and only those being struck by the hammers, as the keys are depressed, are temporarily free of the dampers. With the sustaining pedal depressed, all the dampers are raised, and therefore all the strings are able to vibrate freely. When a note is now struck, its upper partials (i.e. the harmonic series) are reinforced as the strings concerned vibrate in sympathy and thereby add their resonance to the fundamental. It is for this reason that the pedal is sometimes called the 'loud' or 'forte' pedal.

The player can control the amount of resonance of any note or chord – and thus its tone quality and carrying power – by the timing in depressing and raising the pedal. The greatest resonance is obtained when the pedal is depressed before a note or chord is struck. When it is depressed after the keys, the sound is still full but somewhat less sonorous. This is useful for giving resonance to the first note of a phrase, or to detached notes or chords; and in these cases it is important to remember that, just as the pedal goes *down* at the same moment as the fingers, it must also come *up* simultaneously with the fingers, or very nearly so.

Right-hand balance

Balance between hands

The most common type of pedalling is 'syncopated' pedalling. Here the pedal is depressed fractionally after the keys and is raised immediately a new note or chord begins to sound, at which point the process may be repeated. The split-second overlapping of sounds that result from this type of pedalling produces a legato effect similar to that obtained by the 'overlapping' technique using only the fingers as earlier described. But we must never forget that the pedal is a far more potent mechanism than the fingers for sustaining sounds. The two elements must always be carefully co-ordinated. Excellent finger-work can all too easily be wrecked by inefficient or over-enthusiastic pedalling.

This is especially true in the lower registers of the piano, since the lower the note, the greater will be the effect of the pedal. In general terms, the pedal can be depressed earlier and for a longer period for notes in the high register than for those in the middle and low registers, without the sounds becoming obtrusive or blurring with each other. The acoustics of the instrument, as well as those of the hall, will be a decisive factor in determining the minute differences in timing that are required.

It is, of course, possible and sometimes desirable to pedal through a group of notes, providing this does not interfere with a change of harmony or the ending of a phrase. In passage-work, for example, we can greatly enhance the flow of the line by giving a dab of pedal at the peak of a phrase. Rhythmic pedalling on the beat is always to be avoided in this context, but in sequential passages selective pedalling through a group of notes, varying the choice from one sequence to the next, can be particularly effective. Discreet pedalling can also usefully assist a gradual crescendo in both loud and soft passages. However, the pedal should never be held down through rests or staccato notes unless for special effects (although a common fault is to take the hand and foot off together, leaving small gaps of silence between phrases, which disjoints the music). Remember also that the occasional total absence of pedal in a passage is in itself often a striking effect.

Beyond such generalities, the use of the pedal will always be highly subjective. In music of the Romantic period and later it is clearly a necessary ingredient for both technical and interpretative reasons, as its use cannot be specifically marked by the composer. Without the sustaining pedal one simply cannot achieve the luminous quality of sound required in a Chopin Nocturne or the impressionistic sense of '*Dans une brume doucement sonore*' called for by Debussy in his prelude *La cathédrale engloutie*. In Classical and earlier music it is a valuable means of colouring and sustaining the tone, in other words making the piano 'sing'. However for legato playing in such music, my own preference is to rely primarily on finger-work ('overlapping' and 'balancing' techniques), with the pedal as a necessary adjunct. One must beware, incidentally, of composers' own pedal markings in some eighteenth-century music. They were valid for the instruments of the time when the pedal had only recently been introduced, but are not always to be taken literally on the much more resonant instruments of today.

One word about foot technique. While the heel rests on the floor, taking the weight of the leg, the ball of the foot should remain in constant contact with the pedal. The pedal is normally depressed swiftly but without using too much force – certainly without stamping. When allowed to rise, it must always rise sufficiently for the dampers to make full contact with the strings. In syncopated pedalling the rise is quick and the damping sudden. But one can also allow the pedal to rise more slowly so that the damping is gradual, as in the case of a long-held note or chord. The term 'half-pedalling' is often applied to the technique of partial damping, when the depressed pedal is allowed to rise momentarily and insufficiently for the dampers to be fully effective. Correctly used, this technique will allow a bass note struck once to continue sounding, while notes in the upper register – moving chords, for example, played by both hands – are damped. Sustained 'pedal points' can, of course, be obtained more efficiently and in any register by the use of the middle or sostenuto pedal, when a piano is fitted with this useful device. The use of the *Una Corda* should be handled with care. Commonly called the 'soft pedal' (as each hammer strikes only two strings, instead of three, giving a softer and more veiled character to the sound), this pedal should never be used as a mere substitute for *piano* and *pianissimo* touch.

*

To end this section on craftsmanship, here are some words of wisdom for practising:

Bacon said: 'The lame man who keeps the right road outstrips the runner who takes a wrong one.' Stephen Heller said: 'Practise very slowly, progress very fast'; one might add: 'Practise very fast, progress very slowly.'

Musicianship

Now to return to the second aspect of training – learning to become a fine musician.

When a composer is inspired to compose, he gives us not only the notes, but also some clues as to how to play them. A musical pianist is a musical detective, able to spot all the clues. One of the first clues, though frequently overlooked, is the title. All too often I have adjudicated at music festivals and discovered to my dismay that some competitors have not known the title of the piece they are playing. Or even if they knew the title – for example, a mazurka – they did not know what a mazurka is or what are its special characteristics. We should teach young pianists to investigate all the basic clues including the title, tempo indications, key signatures, dynamics, phrase marks, accents and silences (which, as Erwin Stein said, are as important as sounds; Schnabel maintained that many pianists played the notes as well as he did, but it was his silences, pauses and rests which stood his playing apart). They must learn how vital it is to follow and memorise the composer's markings; for to ignore any one of them is to commit a musical crime. Of course, it is a feat to memorise every marking, but if the student has what I call 'musical integrity' they will try remember everything down to the last staccato dot – particularly in Beethoven and Brahms, who were so painstaking in their phrasing and dynamic markings. These clues are the points of departure at the beginning of every musical journey.

All players are entrusted with the works composers have written for their instruments. It is as if they have personally received a legacy under each composer's will: Beethoven's 32 Sonatas, Chopin's 4 Ballades and Bach's 48 Preludes and Fugues – to name but three examples – are the priceless inheritance of every musician. That inheritance carries with it a responsibility to the composer, and a further responsibility to the audience. Every musician is not only the Beneficiary but also the Trustee of the composer's Will. Only through musical integrity, imagination and musical personality can the pianist fulfil that dual responsibility in their re-creation of these great musical masterpieces.

Of course, there will always be the problem of interpreting the short-hand of musical notation. It is impossible to define exactly how slow is *adagio*, how leisurely is an *andante* or *andantino* or how much faster *più allegro* should be than the preceding *allegro*. (I tell my pupils, 'How much *più* is up to you.') It is equally impossible to define exactly how soft is soft, how loud is loud, how much emphasis to put on a *sfortzando*. This piano softness is not the sound of a mother singing a lullaby to a baby, but the carrying sound of a great singer whose *cantabile* can be heard at the back of a large hall. Great thought must be given to the tempi indications and dynamics, their sonorities and textures. The same dynamic produces a different quality of sound in the different registers of the keyboard. Children love the story of the Three Bears when you tell the story using three different registers of voice: 'And Father said [in a very deep voice], "Who's been eating my porridge?"; Mother said [in a higher voice], "Who's been eating my porridge?"; and Baby Bear said [in a high, shrill voice], "Who's been eating my porridge, and eaten it all up?"' and it is the same on the piano, as we can demonstrate, where each register has a different timbre.

I encourage my pupils to compare these different timbres to those of the orchestra: the piano sound in a low register resembles the tone of a double bass and cello, the viola in the middle register, or the bell-like tone of the violin in the high register. Indeed, the pianist should sometimes imagine the piano to be an orchestra – sonatas to be symphonies – and try to imitate the sounds of different instruments. Beethoven Sonatas are full of quartet writing (the E major Sonata Op. 14 No. 1, for example, which Beethoven himself arranged as a string quartet). Bülow, in his edition of Beethoven's Sonatas, marks passages 'Quasi Clarionet', 'Quasi Horn', and used to advise pupils to imitate Joachim's violin tone. Alternatively we can think of vocal timbre: in several of the slow movements from Mozart's Piano Concertos the melodic line can be compared to an aria in one of his operas.

Music cannot exist without melody. It is essentially song and the art of singing has influenced composers from the lullaby of the cradle to the elegy of the grave. To play a simple melody with fine tone and rhythm is one of the greatest of our pianistic challenges. Compare a melody to a sentence in speech – not every word is equally important, and only the most meaningful words are emphasised. A speaker can alter the meaning of a sentence by his choice of emphasis, as indicated in this famous quote from *Hamlet*: 'To be, or not to be: that is the question.'

This short phrase consisting of just ten words adopts different shades of meaning according to the timing, length and the degree of emphasis placed on key words: great actors have given much thought to the words in this sentence. Experiment with this sentence yourself, speaking the words out loud: which versions do *you* think have most impact?

> *To* be, or not to be: that is the question.
> To *be*, or not to be: that is the question.
> To be, *or* not to be: that is the question.
> To be, or *not* to be: that is the question.
> To be, or not *to* be: that is the question.
> To be, or not to *be*: that is the question.
> To be, or not to be: *that* is the question.
> To be, or not to be: that *is* the question.
> To be, or not to be: that is *the* question.
> To be, or not to be: that is the *question*.

So too can a musician alter the meaning of a musical phrase. They must be aware of many of its characteristics: which is the lowest note and which the highest; which are the shortest notes and which the longest; does it progress in steps (conjunct motion, as in a Schubert melody) or in leaps (disjunct motion, as in the striving in the first two bars of Beethoven's *Hammerklavier*); are notes repeated and, if so, for what expressive purpose? Equally they must be aware of the position and importance of the phrase and sequence within the larger melodic span.

In comparing a melody to a sentence or line of poetry, I tell students that, as with words, notes must flow – 'like oil', as Mozart said. But, in order to make sense, the punctuation must also be carefully observed.

Here is a sentence without any punctuation: 'King Charles walked and talked half an hour after his head was cut off.'

Now, the same words, with punctuation: 'King Charles walked and talked. Half an hour after, his head was cut off.'

Music must also make sense. Without properly punctuated phrasing, music is just as nonsensical as the unpunctuated sentence about King Charles. Instrumentalists, in fact, tend to use far too many full-stops in their playing, where only commas and semi-colons are necessary. Their understanding of phrasing can be helped considerably by a theoretical knowledge of musical forms, of harmony and of rhythmic structures, together with aural training. But perhaps most importantly, their musicianship will be defined and enhanced by their familiarity with the art of singing and the necessity of breathing (respiration) between phrases.

Just as sentences contain key words, so each melody has a climax – though different artists will naturally have different views on exactly where it should be. (In my very first lesson with Tobias Matthay, I recall him telling me that when playing I must always think rhythmically forward towards the climax and never stand still until the silence at the end of the piece.) Having shaped a melody, the pianist must then make sure that it is balanced with the accompaniment so that it gives the necessary – yet unobtrusive – support. Finally, having gone through all these details with blood, sweat and toil, the performance should still sound uncontrived.

Music is an art fraught with temporal problems. Musicians may only perform in the present in relationship to what has happened in the past and what is about to happen in the future. This thought process must not only be applied to short passages but must be used to give continuity to large sections of a piece. In a sonata movement, for example, the pianist must make sure that there are no seams showing between the first and second subjects (a radical change in tempo is always to be avoided). Then, the development must *be* a development, with its exciting modulations and bigger tonal proportions. And after the recapitulation, the coda must take its due place as the climax of the movement, perhaps, or as a tranquil memory with a tonal level to match. This is what I meant when I referred in the introduction to the need to give each piece 'rhythmic unity as one architectural whole'.

In a performance, we must imagine that we are going on a journey in time. We should know our destination but also be aware of the delights and surprises on the way. It can be a long journey, as in Schubert's D major Sonata, or a short journey, as in the Chopin Prelude in C minor. We can go slowly, as in a Brahms Intermezzo, or run quickly, as in a spirited Scarlatti Sonata. But, whatever the music, we must always keep on moving forward, tonally and rhythmically, and never mark time on one spot or stop, unless a pause is indicated.

A metronome can be useful to set a speed; it can also strengthen the rhythm and prevent running away in quick passages or dragging in slow ones. There is a game which I play with my pupils that shows the difficulty of maintaining a metronomically strict tempo. While I play the opening of a rhythmic piece – say, a march – two pupils, standing back to back, conduct in time to my playing. I then stop playing and they both continue conducting on their own. After a short time they turn round and compare the correlation of their beats: the chance is only a hundred to one that they will still be together. This is a great party game that I learnt from Nicolai Malko, the great Russian conductor.

When we play, we must be aware simultaneously of the basic pulse and of the rhythmic patterns into which it is divided. It would be wonderful if we could have built into our physiques a number of timing devices to cope with flexible pulses and simultaneous rhythmic patterns within. This would be a great improvement on Maelzel's metronome, which can only give us regular beats, and which can easily make us play mechanically. Having said this, I do find that the metronome is useful in checking that the pianist is not deviating from the intended speed, particularly when stopping and starting.

What constitutes a good rhythmic performance? There must be a certain regularity of pulse; but a relentless, metronomic observance of the beat would destroy the living rhythm, as would any artificial deviation from it. Matthay said that rhythm should be bent but never broken. We must encourage students to aim for a buoyant spring in the rhythm, which is the spine of the music, but without unnecessary liberties. There must always be a reason and purpose behind the slight accelerandos and ritardandos in a melody, for example; the magic of an unexpected harmony; the building up and allargando of a climax or the repose of a final statement in the coda of a slow movement – rhythmic licence in such contexts can never be expressed accurately by notation or tempo indication. No two artists can ever perform the same composition in the same way and I doubt if a performer ever gives exactly the same performance each time.

This is not to say that the composers' tempo indications are not of vital importance. Beethoven made up for the lack of performing instructions in eighteenth-century music by making his tempo indication more and more specific. He went in for markings like *Nicht zu geschwind und sehr singbar vorzutragen* (Non troppo vivace e cantabile assai). I strongly advise my pupils to think carefully about these markings and never to imitate other performers' interpretations from a recording that never changes. When a student has studied a work in depth, then I encourage them to listen to as many live performances as possible. One must never, however, ape another artist. Some young musicians today, instead of studying the score in the minutest detail and re-creating the music for themselves, give performances that are a hotch-potch of ideas thrown together from recordings of every pianist under the sun. Beethoven would never have approved of such a method of 'instant' learning. He was such a stickler for detail that, after reprimanding his pupil Czerny for not following the music, he had to apologise the next day: 'You must forgive a composer who would rather have his work performed exactly as it was written, however beautifully you played it in *other* respects.'

Our lives are governed by rhythm – from a watch ticking away the seconds to the 24-hour rhythm of night and day. Somewhere in between is the fundamental rhythm of our heart-beat. It is surely not a coincidence that the normal heart rate of 60–80 pulses per minute is the speed so often chosen by composers for their works. We hear rhythmic patterns every day of our lives – the ticking of a clock, which groups itself into twos, threes or fours, making duple, triple or quadruple time at the listener's will; the telephone ring; windscreen-wipers; galloping horses; the steady dripping of a tap. In music, this grouping of beats forms bars and each group of these forms a phrase; phrases join together to form larger sections such as exposition, development or recapitulation, until the entire movement or work can be seen as a whole, like the panoramic but detailed view from an aeroplane as it comes into land.

Sometimes the bar-lines are important guide-lines, when it is necessary to reveal the recurring first beat of a bar, but sometimes their function is only visual and they must be mentally erased in favour of a more natural and longer flow of rhythmic line.

Each small rhythmic pattern must be learnt precisely from the very beginning of one's musical training. The exact proportions of, for example, a minim and two crotchets (half-note and two quarter-notes) or of a crotchet and two quavers (quarter-note and two eighth-notes) are not in themselves problematic and can be clapped with precision. When the same rhythm is transferred to the keyboard, however, the very mechanics of finger-work create difficulties for the unwary. The result is a surprisingly frequent and widespread incidence of unrhythmical playing, which in turn destroys the expressive content of the music.

Take, for example, the opening of Schubert's 'Wanderer' Fantasy. If the crotchet/quarter-note is shortened here, the first of the two quavers/eighth-notes will be sounded earlier than it should and thus attract an unwanted accent, while the second quaver/eighth-note is lengthened in compensation. Such inaccurate rhythm will destroy the grandeur of the passage. In fact, almost all music rhythm is the skeleton on which the flesh of tonal colour and expression depend.

Dotted rhythms present another all-too-familiar trap. Take the opening of the famous Tchaikovsky Mazurka from his Children's Album Op. 39 (see page 36). Here again tonal colour and rhythm are intimately connected. When the dotted rhythm is apportioned exactly three parts to one, the articulation will automatically be crisp and springy as required to express the spirit and style of the piece.

There are many other traps that the young performer must be warned against. Because of the natural decay of sound on the piano, longer notes

as a general rule have to be played with fuller tone than shorter ones. The tendency to hurry in quick passages should be countered by a sense of playing the notes with more control. (There is always a danger of panicking before a difficult passage. I tell my students, 'Make haste slowly', i.e. to prepare and organise themselves before they come to the passage. Remember that a quick passage is a slow tune played fast.) In a diminuendo passage, the piano keys will be depressed at a progressively slower rate in order to reduce the volume of sound and this all too frequently leads to a slower tempo. The reverse occurs in a crescendo, when the player will naturally tend to hurry. We must also take into account that in a diminuendo there is often a gradual relaxation of tension, and in a crescendo the tension rises. Nicholas Moldavan, who played the viola in the Flonzale Quartet and was also a member of the National Broadcasting Company (NBC) Symphony Orchestra, described Toscanini's crescendos: 'Nobody could build up a crescendo as he did – by holding you back – holding you – holding you. Other conductors didn't know how to do that: they ran away with you: when it comes to the *forte* they haven't anything left. *He* knew how to build it up gradually.'

We have perhaps strayed back from musicianship into craftsmanship, but this in itself shows how ill-defined is the boundary between them. In practical terms, musicians should be aware of fulfilling three roles when they play:

1   The Performer – plays a few phrases.
2   The Listener – listens and stops to recall the sounds and silences they have produced.
3   The Critic – assesses and analyses the playing. Was it too loud, too soft, too quick, too slow? Did the tone, the rhythm, the musical

punctuation and phrasing add up to their expressive intention? Did they follow the score, and where was the magic?

In this context I cannot emphasise enough how important it is for the pianist to make their expressive intention, i.e. their interpretation, absolutely clear to the listener. An American literary critic once advised writers: 'Say what you mean; you will be taken to mean what you say.' Similarly any performer must recognise that a performance is the sum total of what they play and must be communicated to the audience; in fact, to make the listener listen.

The teacher can always help the young pianist over the choice of repertoire. For beginners, we are fortunate to have such a large number of simple pieces by the great composers from which to choose – other instrumentalists are not so lucky. There are many short pieces by Handel in the Aylesford collection, and by Bach in the Anna Magdalena Notebook, the 20 short Preludes, and the two- and three-part Inventions. Then there are the pieces that Leopold Mozart collected for Nannerl and Amadeus and gave to them as presents on their name-day. There are also Amadeus Mozart's own short pieces, composed when he was very young. Schumann, Mendelssohn and Tchaikovsky all composed works specially for children and in the twentieth century we have simple pieces by Bartók, Kabalevsky and Shostakovich, to name but a few.

A detailed list of works for study and performance by more advanced students cannot be attempted here. The choice of repertoire, and the selection of works for a recital programme, will depend as much on individual temperament as on technical ability and experience. However there are a few general points that should be made.

First, it is vital that pianists should be encouraged to study the masterworks of the Baroque period – Bach's Forty-Eight Preludes and Fugues, the Sonatas by Domenico Scarlatti, and so on. There has been a view in recent times that such works should be played only on the instruments for which they were written and not on the modern piano. To follow such a 'purist' view is to deny the pianist an important and rewarding section of the greatest keyboard literature, which will also help their understanding of music written by later composers. Bach's 'Forty-Eight' have, after all, been called the Old Testament for pianists (Beethoven's Sonatas being the New Testament). Their contrapuntal style challenges the pianist to present the different voices with clarity, and with correct balance of hands and expression. The pianist can usefully imagine each part as an instrumental line in an orchestral score, as I mentioned earlier. The 'linear' thinking required in much Baroque music applies equally to many works of the Classical and Romantic periods: music by the Romantic composers is brimful of part-writing. Classical music has a romantic element and Romantic music has a classical element.

Within the huge Baroque repertoire, I would particularly recommend the Scarlatti Sonatas. There are over 500 from which to choose – their emotional range is wider than is often realised, and they include practically every technical problem a pianist has to master, from nimble passage-work and repeated notes to spectacular leaps and octaves. They focus your attention and make you keep your wits about you with the quickest reactions.

The invention of the pianoforte or *Hammerklavier* in the eighteenth century inspired composers to exploit its new expressive possibilities. Its tone was at first small and intimate; less forceful in fact than the harpsichord and spinet which it only gradually replaced. In Haydn's Sonatas we can see the development of the Classical style in parallel with the demand for increasing volume and richer tone from the instruments on which the music was to be realised. His early sonatas are small in scale and intimate in character. As their formal construction grows more spacious, so too does the requirement for greater sonority and expression to match these later instruments.

The rapid development of compositional style in the Classical period has an important consequence for the performer. The essential repertoire is wide enough – Haydn's Sonatas; Mozart's Sonatas, Rondos, Variations and Concertos; Beethoven's Bagatelles, Variations, Sonatas and Concertos. But to understand and perform even one sonata really well, it is essential to know many of them intimately. (This is a case of quantity yielding quality.) In Beethoven's case, for example, one must have knowledge of sonatas from each of his three compositional periods in order to perform those particular sonatas with which one has a temperamental affinity. Incidentally, I do recommend Czerny's studies as an introduction to Beethoven, whose pupil he was. They capture the sound of Beethoven's passage-work and, for all we know, the style of his playing as well.

Familiarity with works in other genres is also helpful. One must know Mozart's operas to play his Piano Concertos, Haydn's String Quartets to play his Sonatas, and Beethoven's Symphonies and String Quartets to play his Sonatas and Concertos.

Simultaneously with the Classical repertoire must come the study of the great Romantic composers: Schubert, Schumann, Chopin, Liszt and Brahms – their miniatures as well as their major works. Every student of the piano must learn the works of the Impressionist School of Fauré, Debussy and Ravel, for here is a unique world of sound, and then on to Bartók, Messiaen, Rachmaninov, Prokofiev and Shostakovich, and other twentieth-century masters up to the present day.

*

Menuhin said that he 'approached every note with anticipation, and left it with regret'.

Artistry and Performance

When I go to a concert fresh, alert and expectant, I sometimes find that, after a time, instead of listening to Beethoven's Op. 110, or Chopin's Second Ballade, my mind is wandering on to other matters:

> 5 lbs of potatoes
> 2 lbs of carrots
> 2 lbs of onions
> 1 lb of tomatoes

What connection can this possibly have with music? There is none. I have focused on tomorrow's shopping expedition to the supermarket; try as I will, I cannot concentrate on the music, which passes over me and becomes incidental.

'To know whether you are enjoying a piece of music or not', wrote Samuel Butler in 1890, 'you must see whether you find yourself looking at the advertisement for Pears Soap at the end of the programme book.'

Why does one switch off like this? And yet, on other occasions, when one is tired and not in the mood for listening to music, why does one find the performance compelling and wish that time could stand still? The answer lies in the performer's artistry – that elusive, almost magical quality that is the hallmark of all great musicians and transcends the boundaries of age, class, language and race to unite us all. Without that elusive, magical quality, no performer can make the listener listen.

Alfred Neuhaus, one of the greatest Russian teachers, asks: 'What must be done to make a performance live? Is it patience, work, suffering, joy, self-sacrifice?' He says: 'It is to play our magnificent piano literature in such a way as to make the hearer like it, to make him love life still more, make his feeling more intense, his longings more acute and give greater depth to his understanding.'

Here is my list of emotions and moods garnered from the piano literature over many years, to which I refer time and time again when teaching; these emotions, and many more, are to be found in the music of the great composers:

charm · tragedy · tranquillity · resignation · happiness and sadness
humour · brilliance · playfulness · anger · fury · loving · romance
threatening · ominous · proud · powerful · noble · agitated · excited
grand · tender · mysterious · joyful · confident · ecstatic · simple
rippling · joking · passionate · dramatic · vivacious · striving
triumphant · questioning · amusing · sparkling · despondent
silence · watery · melancholic · majestic · lyrical · reflective
dreaming · moving and flowing · light · capricious · fire-y
tempestuous · stormy · whimsical.

The performance is the culminating experience of an artist's intensive work. Something extra happens during a performance that never happens during one's practice. A performance compels continuity, courage and greater concentration. An audience is necessary to give the performer that vital inspiration and spontaneity. Rubinstein said that each audience stimulated him afresh, no matter how familiar were the works he was playing – and indeed one of the unique qualities of his playing was always his spontaneity.

Alan Schulmann, a cellist in the NBC Orchestra, talking about one of the greatest teachers of the past, Toscanini, epitomises what I feel about music and its performance: 'When I think of Toscanini's performances, I think of the clarity of texture, architectural unity, his linear sense; his phrases were marvellous arcs. I think of the flexibility, the forward motion, and yet the repose. The ability to milk every note of the phrase with Italian warmth, intelligence and good taste. *And* the electrifying, incisive rhythm. Yet none of the musicians I knew, or who wrote about him could describe the final magic of his performances. He relied on his innate musical sense – "Cantare, non solfeggiare", that is "Sing, don't play exercises".'

This magic cannot be taught but only stimulated. I advise all aspiring performers to develop a wide appreciation of the Arts in general, to listen to as many live performances as possible, to study folk-songs of many cultures, to take part in chamber music and accompany other musicians (especially singers), to sing in a choir, be an active listener in the concert hall, and to learn also to absorb the sights and sounds of everyday life.

Listening to birdsong helps one to understand the sound of many of Beethoven's trills. Messiaen, too, recorded birdsong and used it in his music. Bartók was influenced by the sounds of insects in the night. Think of the rhythmic beat of the wheels of a train – the triplet rhythm done to perfection; feel the lilt of a swing – 6/8 rhythm; observe the to-ing and fro-ing of waves on the shore – directly invoked in such music as Debussy's *L'isle joyeuse* and *La Mer*; savour the silence of night; the tolling of bells . . . all these, recalled at the right moment, will perhaps help to illumine otherwise dull playing.

Something makes people want to perform. I would never urge anyone on to the concert platform who does not wish to be there, and no teacher ever should. But for those who want to perform, the only way to learn the job is to do it. What the teacher must do is to help in creating the most favourable conditions for individual artistry to emerge and flourish. Many aspects of the essential groundwork have been mentioned and the teacher must always be prepared to help the aspiring performer on the practical details of giving a recital (some general tips are included in the chapter following).

When I am asked what qualities a musician must possess to become a great performer, I would answer only half-jestingly: first, you must have inclination and imagination, backed up by application, concentration and determination. There will be perspiration and at times frustration, even tribulation. But with inspiration you will receive appreciation and possibly adulation!

Giving a Recital

Before the date

- open a file labelled with the place and date of the recital, and keep in it all correspondence and details of the engagement;
- inquire about the size of the hall and its acoustics; the make, size and condition of the piano (and types of pedal available); the fee if relevant; the length of the programme required and the type of audience to which you will be playing.

The choice of programme must bear all of this in mind, but perhaps paramount is to know and to woo your audience as did Horowitz and Rubenstein.

Remember

- to include pieces of light-hearted charm and wit and to prepare an encore or two;
- to send promptly all information required by the organisers – programme details, biographical note, photograph, etc.;
- to have timed the duration of the programme in its entirety and of the individual pieces. Write the approximate timings into your music for future reference;
- to make certain you have enough time booked for rehearsal in the hall;
- to organise a page-turner, if required;
- to plan your travelling time-table carefully, allowing for possible transport delays and time to recover after the journey;
- to check dress requirements – lounge suit, black tie or tails (with correct tie!) for men; long or short dress for women;

- to prepare a check-list of items to take with you. Don't forget the concert-file, contract, paper handkerchiefs, nail-file, spare spectacles, flask of coffee, tea or fruit juice for interval and (in winter) gloves or hand warmer;
- to have an early night before the performance.

On the day

- be punctual for rehearsal and performance. Never keep anyone waiting nor leave anything till the last minute, so that you avoid panic and the consequent frayed nerves;
- show courtesy to all the people who help you, especially the conductor. Your return engagement could depend on it;
- never take drugs or alcohol to calm pre-concert nerves: learn to live with them;
- do not alter your usual pre-concert eating habits;
- don't change your programme except for the most compelling reasons;
- rehearse the full range of items in your programme to familiarise yourself with the instrument and the acoustics of the hall;
- awkward turns and repeats should be rehearsed with a page-turner, if you need one;
- before the concert, practise 'key' passages slowly in the Artist's Room to keep the hands supple;
- never leave valuables unattended in the Artist's Room.

On the platform

- try to achieve a rapport with your audience as quickly as possible. A ready, natural smile is a great asset;
- walk on to the platform steadily and walk off swiftly. Notice at the rehearsal any awkward access to avoid tripping up;
- check that the stool is at the right height and does not wobble;

- take your time. Do not play before you and the audience are ready. Wait for silence before you begin;
- never stamp on the floor or bang on the pedals. Sit as straight as possible and do not fidget, snort or pull faces;
- if you have a memory slip, try to conceal it and 'vamp' till you recover. Avoid at all costs having to stop and apologise.

After the recital

- be diplomatic. If you are disappointed with the piano or with audience reaction, do not say so. These can be sensitive areas with concert organisers;
- be courteous. Write a letter of thanks and appreciation after your visit, especially if you have received any hospitality;
- everyone gets both good and bad reviews. Do not be depressed by the latter: it is only one person's opinion;
- don't rest on your laurels – keep on working and be optimistic about your future!

Competitions
(Local, National and International)

The occurrence of music competitions today is so widespread that one could be forgiven for believing that, like taxes and the poor, they had been part of life since the beginning of time. However, as a feature of the musical scene and as regularly recurring events, their burgeoning dates really from the end of the Second World War. Before then, apart from the Chopin at Warsaw – and the Ysaÿe (afterwards the Queen Elisabeth of the Belgians) at Brussels – they were sporadic and few and far between. The first recorded competition seems to have been a two-horse event between Apollo, God of Music, and Marsyas. The jury consisted of the Nine Muses, daughters of the God, who in a proper exhibition of filial duty, decided in favour of their divine father. There was no prize for winning; rather, the loser suffered the penalty of being flayed alive for his temerity in daring to challenge the God. It is somewhat different today, when both the winner and the jury are similarly flayed alive for daring to outrage the sensibilities of the critics.

Another famous example of music competition was the duel between Mozart and Clementi on Christmas Eve 1781. Staged by the Emperor Josef II in Vienna as Christmas entertainment for the Court, the two composers were asked to play a combination of improvisations and some of their own compositions. Whilst Mozart won the 'theme and variations' part of the duel, Clementi – to the surprise of many – won the portion of the duel centred on showmanship. At the end the Emperor was unable to decide who was the better player and declared the duel a draw. Famously Mozart was not particularly gracious about the result and made several unflattering comments about Clementi, dismissing him as 'merely a technician'.

Even Wagner uses the ambience of a singing competition as an essential part of the dramatic action in his opera, *Die Meistersinger von*

Nürnberg. He, of course, was fully and sometimes painfully aware of the essential competitiveness of musical life. Posterity has granted him the title of winner but during his lifetime he was often the loser.

Competition exists in all walks of life from our earliest days onwards; it is inevitable and, more often than not, beneficial. If one applies for a post as secretary and nineteen other people also apply, only one is successful. That is competition.

Local Competitions

In the field of instrumental music, competitions can begin at an early age – from six or seven onwards. There are three elements necessary for success: a gifted child as raw material; involved parents for encouragement, and a skilled and devoted teacher for instruction and inspiration. The benefits of entering a competition for all those taking part are manifold: the *child* or teenager has an incentive here and will make that extra effort, which is so necessary to give polish to a performance; the *parents* can hear the standards achieved by other young players; and *teachers*, if fortunate enough to produce winners, will enhance their reputations and have a feeling of achievement. Doing well in a competition, not necessarily winning, can be an encouraging and enlightening experience for everyone.

Teachers wishing to enter their students for local competitions should examine the syllabuses of different competitions and choose the classes that include fine music to stimulate the young pianist; we are fortunate that many of the great masters wrote gems that are aimed specifically at the young pianist. A competition committee, which gives thought to the repertoire even at an elementary level, will invite more experienced and musical adjudicators. Their adjudication will praise where possible but will also give constructive criticism, which should be noted. Teachers, parents and students should take little notice of the *marks* but great notice of the *remarks* of the adjudicator.

Teachers should avoid sending in more than one student for the same class if possible, as this can incite jealousy and be a bitter experience for all those concerned: students, parents and teacher. If possible encourage the students to participate and prepare the piece in the greatest detail. The point of departure for studying competitive festival pieces is to know

47

and understand the title (I have sometimes adjudicated where a march is played like Dolly's Funeral and a Lullaby jazzes about!). Immediately before the competition itself, students should perform their pieces under performance conditions in front of fellow students, parents and friends to give added confidence and performance continuity. Whatever slips may occur, these must be covered up; the show must go on!

National Competitions

Young winners in local competitions are all too frequently lauded and applauded by relatives and friends who, often with a lack of discerning judgment, have referred to them as geniuses when they are not although, of course, they are highly gifted musicians. They have had a string of successes in local competitions and have been big fishes in little local ponds. They may have changed teachers – for better or for worse – and they may not have the backing of their parents, who are no longer as enthusiastic about music as a career, realising the hazards and insecurity of the profession. The next 'test' for dedicated and determined competitors at this age and stage is to try their luck in a national competition.

The air is rarer here; the standard of playing is much higher, the repertoire is more searching and they often have to give a recital to include masterpieces by Mozart, Beethoven, Chopin, Schumann, Bartók and so on; sometimes they even have freedom of choice. The three aspects of teaching I cover earlier in this book – craftsmanship, musicianship and artistry – become infinitely more important at this stage.

International Competitions

The admission by audition to an international competition is the first hurdle. You may well ask what qualities the jury of an international piano competition is looking for at this stage. I have previously written about the three elements that contribute towards creating a fine pianist. But it is the in-depth reading and comprehension of the score, which I call *musical integrity*, that is now of vital importance.

It is the third and rarest of my fundamentals that is sought by a jury: artistry, which includes musical integrity, i.e. adherence to the score and the composer's instructions; rhythmic vitality, the spine of music; the subtly varied rubato that gives spring to the rhythm and enables a melody to soar; passion; fine sonority and how to make the piano – a percussive instrument – sing; and lastly that indefinable quality called magic, imagination or inspiration, which, I must emphasise again, no teacher can teach.

I am often asked whether the finest artists always win the first prize. I reply that, for example, the jury in the Leeds International Piano Competition, having listened to about nearly one hundred solo recitals and six concertos in nearly three weeks, has come to the conclusion in its musical wisdom that *this* competitor at *this* time and in *this* place shall be proclaimed the winner. However the jury at this time has no access to a crystal ball, which might reveal aspects such as the following:

1   The future personal fortunes and misfortunes of the winner and how they will react to them. They win competitions at a period in their lives when they fall in love, marry, sometimes – unhappily – separate and divorce. These situations and emotional traumas can play havoc with their performances as musicians. We, the members of the Jury, do not know if the winner possesses the necessary great reserves of physical and emotional stamina to overcome these traumas.

2   How do they react to adverse criticism, especially in the Press. Will it depress them, or are they able to shrug it off and keep going?

3   Nerves, which are inevitable and which may have lowered the standard of the performance.

4   How much intensive teaching went into the preparation of the competition programmes, and whether they are dependent on their teacher.

5   How quickly they can absorb and memorise new repertoire at the same time as travelling and performing all over the world.

6   How well they cope with jetlag. Do they enjoy travelling, living out of a suitcase and being away from home, friends and family?

Only the passage of time will tell. Many doors will have been opened by an international competition. With the winner's musical attainments and the professional opportunities provided, giving worldwide exposure, it is hoped that all these musical doors will remain open for the rest of their lives.

I live with the criticism that competitions can do more harm than good. I disagree with this point of view. There is always competition – in life, as well as in any field of artistic endeavour. The aspirant to a prize in a competition has to win only once to realise that they have been cast into the ocean of professional life and that they have to swim very hard to reach for the occasional lifebelts that professional engagements represent. It is only after winning a prize at an international competition that the competition of real life begins – from now on, they are compared to all the great pianists of the past and present, irrespective of age, and not only pianists of their own generation.

For our critics, I would ask, 'What are the alternatives to competitions?' In what I think of as the bad old days, the usual route was through privilege, money or influence. Very occasionally an impresario would take up an artist but it was a very hit-and-miss undertaking. Today if a young artist wants to break into the professional market, the cost of mounting a recital in the capital, advertising it and playing (usually to a pitiful handful of friends and relatives) is almost prohibitive, involving thousands of pounds; and even then, there is no guarantee that an audience will materialise or that the critics of influence will attend, let alone write a favourable review.

Although competitions are very serious professional events, there are one or two anecdotes that are relevant to the competition world. I was serving on the Jury for the Queen's Prize at the Royal College of Music in London, flanked on either side by two eminent colleagues. The candidate started the last movement of Beethoven's Appassionata Sonata too fast for the composer's marking of *Allegro ma non troppo* ('fast, but not too fast'). Surprised, I turned to my colleague on my right and said, 'Don't you think that is too fast?' to which he replied, 'I'm sorry? I'm deaf in my left ear'. Amazed at the admission, I turned to my left and whispered, 'He says he's deaf in his left ear', to which the second juror replied, 'I'm deaf in my right.'

My second story will give you some indication of the difficulty of young pianists trying to make their way in this most challenging and lonely profession. A fine, starving young pianist noticed that the circus was coming to town, so he rang the Director asking for a job. 'Have you any work for a poor, starving pianist?' he asked, 'I play a very fine *Mephisto Waltz*.' 'Sorry, I have no work for a pianist,' the Director replied. After a few days had elapsed and feeling very hungry indeed, he called the Director once again. 'I can play Liszt's *Campanella*, if you prefer?' 'Sorry, I can offer you nothing,' came the reply. At a third attempt to interest the circus Director, he called once more and pleaded, 'I can play the *Mephisto Waltz* and *La Campanella* together, at the same time.' Intrigued, the Director said, 'All right, come along.' At the interview he was told that the performing bear was sick and the pianist was instructed to don a bear skin. He was told that the bear crossed the ring on a tightrope, beneath which prowled and snarled a den of savage lions. 'I have nothing to lose,' thought the starving pianist; so he agreed to walk the tightrope. All went well at first but, halfway across, he lost his balance and fell amongst the lions. 'Oh save me!' he cried, in desperation. *Sotto voce* a whisper from one of the lions said, 'Don't worry; we're all pianists.'

This fantasy alas tells the truth about the music profession today. There are far too many pianists for the number of engagements available.

To give you an idea as to what is required of a competitor at an international piano competition, at 'the Leeds' the three solo rounds are of thirty, fifty-five and seventy-five minutes respectively (all from memory), before the final round of a concerto with orchestra. Other competitions may vary in some respect from our formula. For instance, in Moscow the Tchaikovsky Competition requires two concerti played back to back but dispenses with the seventy-five-minute recital. Other competitions shorten one of the solo rounds and include some chamber music. Some competitions are extremely selective in their pre-selection of candidates, limiting the number of those performing to a mere thirty-five or forty competitors; whereas we, at 'the Leeds', believing that you have to have a lot of milk for a little cream, admit about a hundred *and* give them thirty minutes each in the first stage. From all of this, it will be immediately recognised that one quality that is essential for success in music competitions is stamina.

Looking back over my musical career of more than sixty-five years and to the many young talents entrusted to me, I am deeply grateful to them for this privilege. I enjoy my teaching as much as ever, for my pupils are my true friends and lifeblood. They have taught me as much as I have taught them, as there is no age at which I believe one can stop learning. The fine competitors I have heard across the world have been an inspiration to me for their humility, and consummate artistry and dedication.

*

After hearing Murray Perahia in his debut recital in 1972 at the Queen Elizabeth Hall, Sir Clifford Curzon wrote to me and said: 'What greater pleasure is there in life than giving a young and beautiful talent a little lift in the direction of the stars although he may never reach them?' This is the ethos of 'the Leeds'.

Rules and Maxims for Young Musicians *

ROBERT SCHUMANN (1810–1856)

- The cultivation of the ear is of the greatest importance. Endeavour, in good time, to distinguish tones and keys. The bell, the window-shutter, the cuckoo – try to find out in what key are the sounds these produce.

- You must industriously practise scales and other finger exercises. There are people, however, who think they may attain to everything in doing this; until a ripe age they daily practise mechanical exercises for many hours. That is as reasonable as trying to pronounce 'a, b, c' quicker and quicker every day. Make a better use of your time.

- Play in time! The playing of some virtuosos resembles the walk of a drunken man. Do not make such your models.

- Dragging and hurrying are equally great faults.

- Try to play easy pieces well; it is better than to play difficult ones in a mediocre style.

- If you have finished your daily musical work, and feel tired, do not force yourself to further labour. It is better to rest than to practise without pleasure or freshness.

- Do not try to attain mere technical facility, the so-called bravura. Try to

* Extracts from *Music and Musicians, essays and criticisms by Robert Schumann* (published 1877). Translated Fanny Raymond Ritter.

produce the same impression with a composition, as that which the composer aimed at; no one should attempt more; anything beyond it is mere caricature.

- Lose no opportunity of playing music, duos, trios, etc., with others. This will make your playing broader and more flowing. Accompany singers often.

- People live on the other side of the mountain too. Be modest! You never thought of or invented anything that others had not already thought of or invented before you. And even if you had done so, you should consider it a gift from above, which you ought to share with others.

- If you pass a church while the organ is being playing, go in and listen. If you long to sit on the organ-bench yourself, try your little fingers, and wonder at this great musical power.

- Sing in choruses industriously, especially the middle voices. This will make you a good reader, and intelligent as a musician.

- What is it to be intelligently musical? You are not so when, with eyes painfully fastened on the notes, you laboriously play a piece through; you are not so when you stop short and find it impossible to proceed, because some one has turned over two pages at once. But you are so when, in playing a new piece, you almost foresee what is coming, when you play an old one by heart; in short, when you have taken music not only into your fingers, but into your head and heart.

- How may we become musical in that sense? Dear child, the principal requisites, a fine ear and a swift power of comprehension, come, like all things, from above. But this foundation must be improved and increased. You cannot do this by shutting yourself up all day like a hermit, and practising mechanical exercises, but through a vital, many-sided musical activity, and especially through familiarity with chorus and orchestra.

- Listen attentively to all folk songs; these are a treasure of lovely melodies, and will teach you the characteristics of different nations.

- Observe the tone and character of the different instruments; try to impress their peculiar tone-colours on your ear.

- Honour the old, but bring a warm heart to what is new. Do not be prejudiced against unknown names.

- Do not judge a composition on a first hearing of it; that which pleases most at first is not always the best. Masters must be studied. Many things will only become clear to you when you are old.

- You should early learn to conduct; observe good conductors; when alone, practise conducting occasionally. This will help you in becoming clear regarding the compositions you are studying.

- You are certain to rise through industry and perseverance.

- From a pound of iron, that costs only a few pence, many thousand watch-springs, the value of which runs into the hundreds of thousands, may be made. Faithfully use the pound heaven has entrusted to you.

- Study is unending.